Kelpie's BELLS

Written by
Irene Javors

Illustrated and
designed by
Matthew Snow

4

m   elpie.

I am a Manx cat. Manx cats are different from other cats. Manx cats are born with no

t
  a
    i
      l.

But

while

I

do not have a

t a i l

I

do

have

a t a l e

to tell.

I am a purfectly Happy Cat

living with my person in a wonderful house.

My life is like clockwork. Nothing ever changes.

12 1 2 3 4 5 6 7 8 9 10 11

I feel
safe
and
secure.

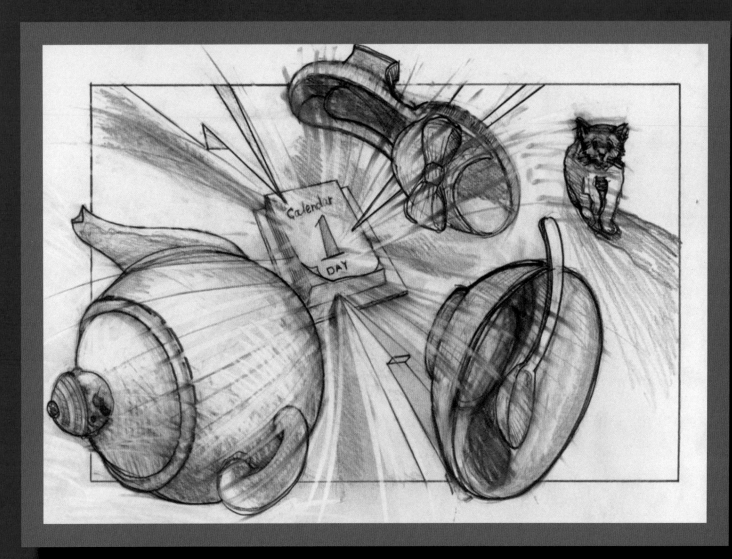

Then
one
day,
without
warning,

disaster

strikes!

We move!

We move into a strange house.
Everything is strange.

And worst of all
a new person has
moved in with
US!

Everyone is busy
moving furniture
and talking and
no one is paying

any attention to me.

I don't feel loved !

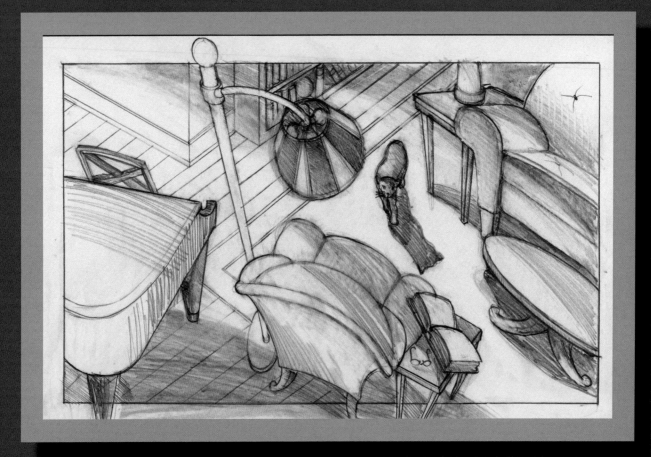

I slink off to find a chair to settle in where I can lick my paws and feel sorry for myself.

"Where's EKl ppie?"

They ask.
They look
around and
see I'm
in my
chair.

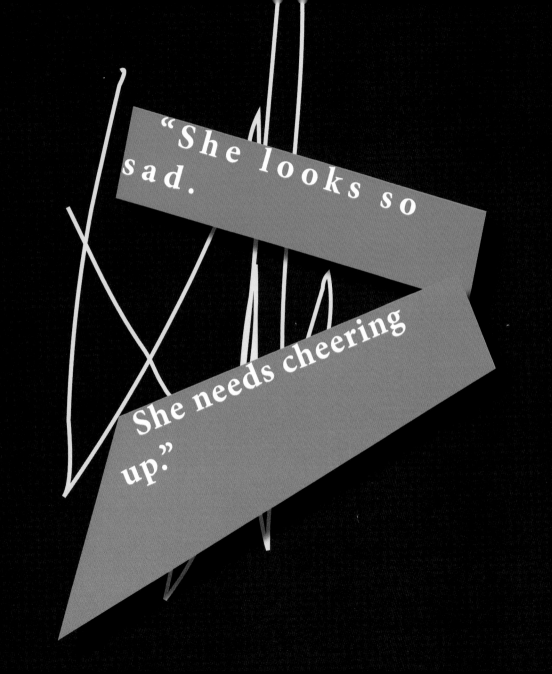

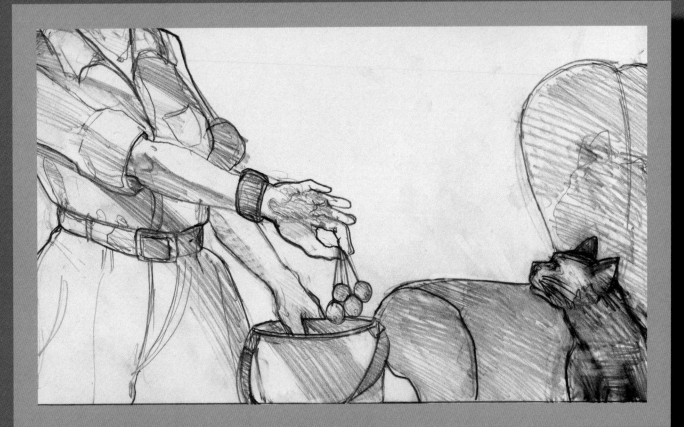

"I have an idea," the new person says.
She takes some things out of her purse

and

shakes

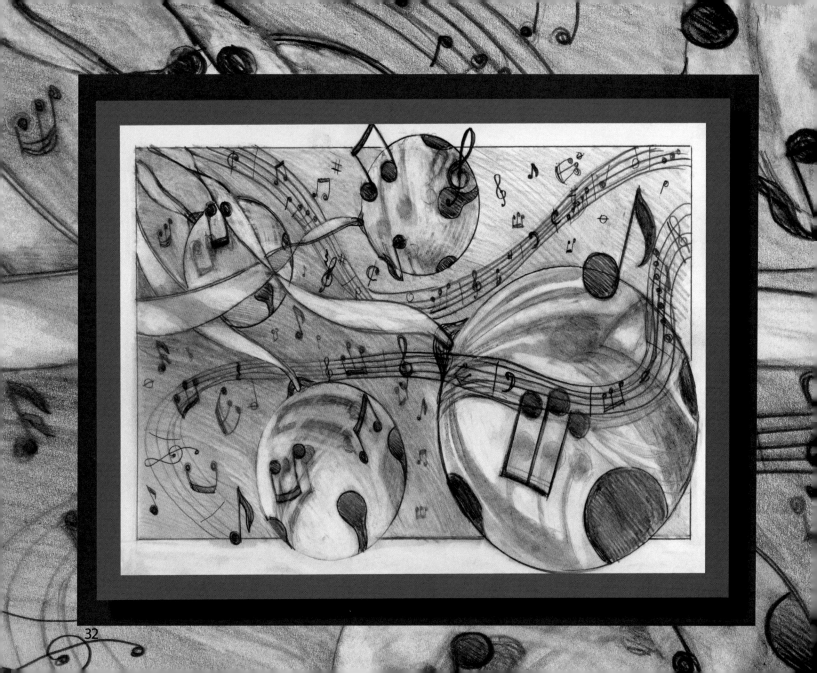

She pins them to my chair
and I swat at them.

She laughs!

I ring them again.

It is a song - a song of love and friendship.

Irene Javors, LMHC,
has degrees in counseling,
philosophy and history. She
writes about the interface
between culture and psyche.
She is the human campanion
for two felines.

Matthew Snow
is a designer and
illustrator. He lives
and works in NYC.
He loves dogs as
well as cats and is
the human companion
to a papillon.